FORGOTTEN FACTS ABOUT

LIFE IN THE WILD WEST

BY KATHLEEN CONNORS

Enslow PUBLISHING

HISTORY'S FORGOTTEN FACTS

Please visit our website, www.enslow.com. For a free color catalog of all our high-quality books, call toll free 1-800-398-2504 or fax 1-877-980-4454.

Library of Congress Cataloging-in-Publication Data
Names: Connors, Kathleen, author.
Title: Forgotten facts about life in the wild West / Kathleen Connors.
Description: Buffalo, New York : Enslow Publishing, [2024] | Series: History's forgotten facts | Includes bibliographical references and index.
Identifiers: LCCN 2023029109 | ISBN 9781978537736 (library binding) | ISBN 9781978537729 (paperback) | ISBN 9781978537743 (ebook)
Subjects: LCSH: Frontier and pioneer life–West (U.S.)–Juvenile literature. | West (U.S.)–Social conditions–19th century–Juvenile literature. | Cowboys–West (U.S.)–History–19th century–Juvenile literature.
Classification: LCC F596 .C736 2024 | DDC 978.02–dc23/eng/20230705
LC record available at https://lccn.loc.gov/2023029109

Published in 2024 by
Enslow Publishing
2544 Clinton Street
Buffalo, NY 14224

Portions of this work were originally authored by Arthur K. Britton and published as *Life in the Wild West.* All new material in this edition authored by Kathleen Connors.

Designer: Tanya Dellaccio Keeney
Editor: Kristen Rajczak Nelson

Photo credits: Cover, series background (banners) Ledelena/Shutterstock.com; cover, series background (paper) Vitaly Korovin/Shutterstock.com; cover, series background (wood) Pataradon Luangtongkum/Shutterstock.com; cover duncan1890/iStock.com; pp. 4, 7 Everett Collection/Shutterstock.com; p. 5 https://upload.wikimedia.org/wikipedia/commons/4/40/United_States_1850-1853-03.png; p. 8 https://upload.wikimedia.org/wikipedia/commons/e/e6/Black_Sheriff.jpg; p. 9 camaralenta/iStock.com; p. 10 https://upload.wikimedia.org/wikipedia/commons/d/d1/HerdQuit.jpg; p. 11 https://upload.wikimedia.org/wikipedia/commons/8/82/Cattle_Roundup%2C_Great_Falls%2C_MT%2C_Geo_B_Bonnell%2C_c1890.jpg; p. 13 https://upload.wikimedia.org/wikipedia/commons/0/01/Billy_the_Kid_tintype%2C_Fort_Sumner%2C_1879-80-Edit2.jpg; p. 15 meunierd/Shutterstock.com; p. 16 https://upload.wikimedia.org/wikipedia/commons/3/32/Young-Man-Afraid-of-His-Horses_%28Tashun-Kakokipa%29%2C_an_Oglala_Sioux%2C_standing_in_front_of_his_lodge%2C_Pine_Ridge%2C_South_Dak_-_NARA_-_530813.jpg; p. 17 (Nez Perce) Courtesy of the Library of Congress; p. 17 (Apache) https://upload.wikimedia.org/wikipedia/commons/7/76/William_S._Soule_-_Pacer.jpg; p. 19 (Annie Oakley) https://upload.wikimedia.org/wikipedia/commons/0/05/Annie_Oakley_Portrait.jpg; p. 19 (Buffalo Bill) https://upload.wikimedia.org/wikipedia/commons/f/f8/Buffalo_Bill_Cody_ca1875.jpg; p. 19 (Frank Butler) https://upload.wikimedia.org/wikipedia/commons/2/27/Frank_E_Butler_c1882.png.

Printed in the United States of America

CPSIA compliance information: Batch #CWENS24: For further information contact Enslow Publishing at 1-800-398-2504.

CONTENTS

Words in the glossary appear in **bold** type the first time they are used in the text.

WHERE AND WHEN

When people picture the Wild West, they might imagine cowboys riding into the sunset. They may think of shoot-outs and battles with Native Americans. While some of this happened, other truths of the Wild West have been forgotten!

MANY PLACES THOUGHT OF AS PART OF THE WILD WEST WEREN'T U.S. STATES YET. THAT OFTEN MEANT THERE WERE FEW LAWS. THAT'S WHY IT WAS CALLED WILD!

UNITED STATES, 1850

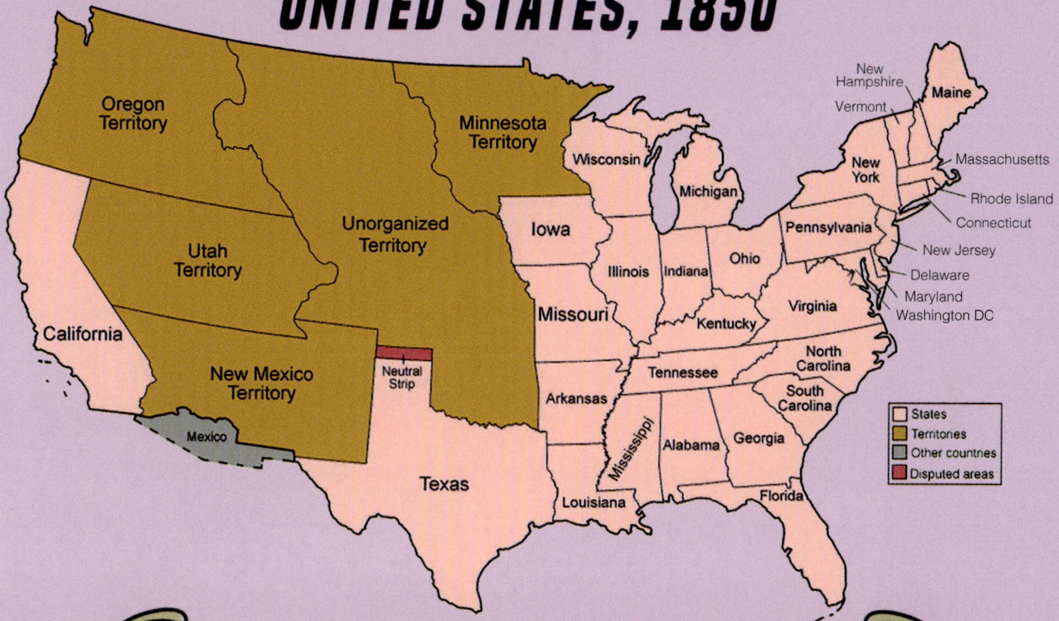

DON'T FORGET!

The time of the Wild West started during the 1850s and ended around 1900 or a bit after.

Some historians, or people who study history, say the Wild West was the area from the Mississippi River to the Pacific Ocean. Others only include areas near the Rocky Mountains, such as Montana, down to Texas and the West Coast.

THE QUIET LIFE

Many people headed west to get rich after some men found gold in California in 1848. Others set up **ranches** and farms in the western **territories**. They had to work hard to build their own homes. They had to grow and make all their own food.

That doesn't sound too wild! It may have been a quiet life for many. It was often lonely. Some homes were many miles from a town. Still, in some places, people fought over **resources** such as gold.

THE CALIFORNIA GOLD RUSH MAY HAVE BROUGHT MANY PEOPLE WEST, BUT FEW GOT RICH BY FINDING GOLD!

DON'T FORGET!

Disease, or illness, caused many deaths in the Wild West. Illnesses caused by poor **sanitation** were common.

HOME ON THE RANGE

In movies of the Wild West, cowboys have often all been white men. In fact, many real cowboys were Native American, Black, and Mexican! Mexican cowboys were called vaqueros (vah-KEHR-ohz).

BLACK AMERICANS HAD OTHER JOBS IN THE WILD WEST TOO. THIS MAN WAS A SHERIFF, OR LAWMAN, IN IDAHO.

DON'T FORGET!

American cowboys learned much of what they needed to know from the vaqueros. "Buckaroo," another name for a cowboy, came from the word vaquero.

THE COWBOY HAT CAME FROM THE SOMBRERO WORN BY VAQUEROS! THESE WERE LARGE HATS VAQUEROS WORE TO BLOCK THE SUN.

There's no question that cowboys had to be brave and strong—just like in stories of the Wild West. Cowboys' lives were hard. They worked long hours and didn't make much money. They either slept on the ground or in **bunkhouses** as they moved from ranch to ranch.

DRIVING CATTLE

Cowboys herded cattle from Texas to Kansas each spring. The cattle drive, or trail drive, took about three months. Cowboys rode all day and took turns at night watching the cattle. They cared for sick and hurt cattle, helped cows have their babies, and searched for lost cattle.

DON'T FORGET!

Cowboys didn't do much for fun at the end of the day. They were so tired from work that they went to bed early.

COWBOYS ON A CATTLE DRIVE ATE BEANS, BACON, BISCUITS, AND RICE. THEY WORE THE SAME CLOTHES EVERY DAY.

In addition, cowboys faced storms, range fires, cattle **rustlers**, and, sometimes, angry Native Americans. If cattle **stampeded,** cowboys had to ride ahead of them to stop them. Driving cattle was hard, dangerous work.

GETTING WILD!

Some stories of the West are wild—and true! Gunfights did happen, especially in Texas. There were more than 150 that occurred there between the 1860s and the 1890s. Outlaws such as Jesse James and his brother, Frank, robbed banks and trains.

Other stories are less wild than has been remembered. The gunfight at O.K. **Corral** in Tombstone, Arizona, lasted only about 30 seconds—and it didn't even take place in the O.K. Corral! However, three men were killed.

BILLY THE KID BECAME AN OUTLAW AROUND AGE 15! LAWMEN JAILED HIM FOR TAKING PART IN A THEFT, BUT HE ESCAPED. LATER, HE WAS WANTED FOR KILLING SOMEONE AND STEALING A HORSE.

DON'T FORGET!

Dodge City, Kansas, became known as a lawless **symbol** of the Wild West. It was only truly wild for about a year—but in that time, 18 men were killed by gunshot!

SOME LAW

In towns of the Wild West, settlers set up their own law **enforcement**. Wyatt Earp was a lawman in many places, including Dodge City. He was also a buffalo hunter and a gunfighter. Wyatt was often in trouble with the law too! He was said to have stolen money and horses.

In places with few lawmen, vigilantes turned up. Vigilantes sometimes killed the people they caught without waiting for the crime to be proven.

DON'T FORGET!

A vigilante is someone who is not officially part of law enforcement but works to find and punish those they believe have committed crimes.

WYATT EARP WANTED TO BE THOUGHT OF AS A GREAT HERO. HE TOLD MANY STORIES ABOUT HIS BRAVERY AND DEEDS THAT WEREN'T TRUE!

NATIVE NATIONS

It's true that Native Americans and settlers in the Wild West fought. But, in old stories of the Wild West, Native Americans were shown as the "bad guys." That's not the whole story!

DON'T FORGET!

The United States forced Native groups in the West to live on reservations. A reservation is an area of land set aside for Native Americans.

MEMBER OF THE LAKOTA NATION

SOME OF THE NATIVE AMERICAN NATIONS HARMED BY THE WESTERN SETTLEMENT OF WHITE AMERICANS WERE THE NEZ PERCE, THE APACHE, AND THE LAKOTA, AMONG OTHERS.

MEMBERS OF THE NEZ PERCE NATION

MEMBER OF THE APACHE NATION

Native Americans had lived in the West for thousands of years. There were many different nations with different ways of life. When the U.S. government and settlers took their land, these groups fought back. They wanted to keep their people safe and continue their way of life.

A TRAVELING TALE

Some of the tales about how wild the Wild West was come from newspapers of the time **exaggerating** the truth. They just wanted to sell more papers!

Other imagined ideas of the Wild West were born from Buffalo Bill's traveling Wild West show. It started in 1883 and had cowboys, Native Americans, and action-packed plays. Writers who had never seen the West made up tales that had wild, mean Native Americans and few Black people, Mexicans, and women.

BUFFALO BILL'S SHOW MADE PEOPLE LIKE ANNIE OAKLEY (LEFT) FAMOUS! OAKLEY AND HER HUSBAND, FRANK BUTLER (RIGHT) BECAME KNOWN FOR THEIR SHOOTING SKILLS.

DON'T FORGET!

William Cody, known as Buffalo Bill, brought in real cowboys from the Wild West to perform in his shows. They rode broncos, or wild horses, and showed off roping skills later used in **rodeos**.

LOOKING BACK

Art made during the time of the Wild West often wanted to show the good of westward **expansion**. It ignored harm to Native Americans. Movies made from about 1920 until the 1950s showed the Wild West as a place of brave heroes, evil outlaws, and adventure.

Today, historians study forgotten facts, such as how poorly women, Black Americans, and Native Americans were treated. These facts are less *wild*—but knowing the truth about history allows us to learn from it!

DATES TO REMEMBER

1848
THE DISCOVERY OF GOLD IN CALIFORNIA BRINGS PEOPLE WEST.

1866
THE FIRST CATTLE DRIVE TAKES PLACE.

JESSE AND FRANK JAMES ROB THEIR FIRST BANK.

1875
BILLY THE KID COMMITS HIS FIRST CRIME.

1881
THE GUNFIGHT AT THE O.K. CORRAL TAKES PLACE.

1883
BUFFALO BILL'S WILD WEST SHOW BEGINS.

1885
CATTLE DRIVES END.

DON'T FORGET!

Belle Starr and Pearl Heart were women outlaws! They challenged the idea that women of the time would only stay home and care for children and their house.

GLOSSARY

bunkhouse: A place for workers to sleep.

corral: A pen for livestock.

enforcement: Making sure that people are doing what they are expected to do.

exaggerate: To think of or describe something as larger or greater than it really is.

expansion: Having to do with getting larger.

ranch: A large farm for raising cattle or horses.

resource: A usable supply of something.

rodeo: A contest of many events involving cowboy skills.

rustler: Someone who steals cattle.

sanitation: Having to do with actions taken for health and cleanliness.

stampede: To run wildly in panic.

symbol: Something that stands for something else.

territory: Land that belongs to a government.

FOR MORE INFORMATION

Books

Bearce, Stephanie. *Awesome, Disgusting, Unusual Facts About the Wild West*. Mankato, MN: Black Rabbit Books, 2024.

London, Martha. *Fact and Fiction of the Wild West.* Minneapolis, MN: Abdo Publishing, 2022.

Websites

Cowboy Facts for Kids
www.theclassroom.com/cowboy-kids-8171301.html
Check out fun facts about cowboys here.

Native American Facts for Kids
www.native-languages.org/kids.htm
Find out more about the many different groups of Native people of North America.

Publisher's note to educators and parents: Our editors have carefully reviewed these websites to ensure that they are suitable for students. Many websites change frequently, however, and we cannot guarantee that a site's future contents will continue to meet our high standards of quality and educational value. Be advised that students should be closely supervised whenever they access the internet.

INDEX